Johannes Brahms

GERMAN REQUIEM

IN FULL SCORE

From the Breitkopf & Härtel Complete Works Edition
Edited by Eusebius Mandyczewski

DOVER PUBLICATIONS, INC., NEW YORK

Published in Canada by General Publishing Company, Ltd.,
30 Lesmill Road, Don Mills, Toronto, Ontario.
Published in the United Kingdom by Constable and Company, Ltd.,
10 Orange Street, London, WC2H 7EG.

This Dover edition, first published in 1987, is a republication of Volume 17 (*Ein deutsches Requiem nach Worten der heiligen Schrift für Soli, Chor und Orchester [Orgel ad libitum], Op. 45*) of *Johannes Brahms; Sämtliche Werke; Ausgabe der Gesellschaft der Musikfreunde in Wien*, originally published by Breitkopf & Härtel, Leipzig, n.d. (Editor's Preface dated Spring 1926). A new table of contents, a new English list of instruments and voices, and a new English translation of the *Revisionsbericht* (Editor's Commentary) have been added, as well as the King James Version passages of the Bible corresponding to the German vocal texts.

Manufactured in the United States of America
Dover Publications, Inc., 31 East 2nd Street, Mineola, N.Y. 11501

Library of Congress Cataloging-in-Publication Data

Brahms, Johannes, 1833–1897.
[Deutsches Requiem]
German requiem.

For soprano, bass, chorus, and orchestra.
German words.
Reprint. Originally published: Leipzig :
Breitkopf & Härtel, 1926?
(Sämtliche Werke / Johannes Brahms ; Bd. 17)
With new English translation of the editorial commentary.
English translation of words printed as text: p.
1. Requiems. I. Mandyczewski, Eusebius. II. Title.
M2010.B8 op.45   1987   87-751281
ISBN 0-486-25486-0

Contents

Editor's Commentary   vii

Revisionsbericht   xi

Instrumentation   xiii

Vocal Texts (German and English)   xiv

1. *Chorus:* Selig sind, die da Leid tragen   3

2. *Chorus:* Denn alles Fleisch es ist wie Gras   21

       Die Erlöseten des Herrn   42

3. *Bass Solo and Chorus:* Herr, lehre doch mich   60

4. *Chorus:* Wie lieblich sind deine Wohnungen   95

5. *Soprano Solo and Chorus:* Ihr habt nun Traurigkeit   114

6. *Baritone Solo and Chorus:* Denn wir haben hie keine
       bleibende Statt   127

       Denn es wird die Posaune schallen   136

       Herr, du bist würdig   150

7. *Chorus:* Selig sind die Toten   172

Editor's Commentary

The following sources in the collection of the Gesellschaft der Musikfreunde in Vienna served for our edition:

A. the composer's autograph;
B. the first edition, composer's personal copy;
C. the parts used for the first Viennese performances under the direction of the composer.

A. The autograph, written on seven "signatures" (one for each movement) in vertical format, carries on the first page the brief title: **"Ein deutsches Requiem. J.B."**

First movement: Twelve leaves of fourteen-staff paper; after the ninth leaf an inserted leaf of eighteen-staff paper with the later changes. Title: "Selig sind, die da Leid tragen."

Second movement: Twelve leaves of twenty-staff paper; four leaves of twenty-staff paper of another format; four leaves of eighteen-staff paper; after the sixteenth leaf a half-leaf as an addition with the later changes. Title: "Denn alles Fleisch ist wie Gras."

Third movement: Eighteen leaves of twenty-staff paper. Title: "Herr, lehre doch mich."

Fourth movement (originally labeled as no. 5): Twelve leaves of eighteen-staff paper. Title: "Wie lieblich sind deine Wohnungen."

Fifth movement: eight leaves of eighteen-staff paper. Title: "Ihr habt nun Traurigkeit."

Sixth movement: Eight leaves of eighteen-staff paper; twenty-four leaves of twenty-staff paper. Title: "Denn wir haben hie."

Seventh movement: Fourteen leaves of twenty-staff paper. Title: "Selig sind die Todten." At the end the composer notes: "Baden-Baden im Sommer 1866."

The titles derived from the opening words of the individual movements were deleted by the publisher, surely only with the consent of the composer; the publisher also gave directions for engraving on the first page, and completed the text of all the movements where it was not yet self-evident. Thus the autograph was able to serve as the engraving copy, as is also apparent from the indicated division into plates. In this source the vocal parts are written in the vocal clefs, and the parts for the instruments to be used ad libitum are lacking—that is, contrabassoon and organ, whose entrances were only later indicated by the composer.

B. The first edition appeared in 1868, published by Rieter-Biedermann (now C. F. Peters) in Leipzig under the title "Ein deutsches Requiem nach Worten der Heiligen Schrift für Soli, Chor und Orchester (Orgel ad libitum) von Johannes Brahms op. 45. Partitur. Klavierauszug mit Text. Klavierauszug zu vier Händen. Chor- und Orchesterstimmen," with the publication numbers 592–596. In the full score the organ part is missing; the organ's entrances and exits are indicated in the double-bass part by "Org. t. s.," "con Org.," "Org. tacet." But a completely worked-out organ part is included with the orchestral parts. In contrast, neither the full score nor the parts show any sign of the contrabassoon. However, in his personal copy of the score the composer later indicated in blue pencil the entrances and exits of this instrument; "c. Vc.," "c. B.," "tac." show where and how long it proceeds along with the cello or double bass.

C. The old Viennese orchestral parts used by the composer contain a notated contrabassoon part corresponding with the indications in the above-mentioned sources. That it is not expressly marked as an ad libitum part may have been a careless error of the copier. It is not an obligatory part, as is evident from what has been said and from its nature.

Source A reveals in detail how the composer polished and improved his work even after its completion. It is well known that he never published anything without having heard it first. So the changes in the *German Requiem,* too, may be traced to the effect of the first rehearsals. First, two expansions in the first movement stand out: the ten measures following letter E replaced the five measures shown here (p. ix) as Example 1; and the ten measures that begin at page 17, measure 5, grew out of the seven in Example 2. For the beginning of the second movement, originally only *piano, mezza voce,* and *legato* were stipulated, and for the strings *legato e dolce.* The inadequacy of these directions was surely proven by the rehearsals. The middle section in G-flat major, "Etwas bewegter," was originally without harp. After the repeat of the first part, the B-flat major section (letter H) was to have begun *Un poco animato.* Three measures before letter M, the composer later inserted a measure; our Example 3 shows the original version of this passage. In the third movement, what stands out first is the notation of the clarinets; it was notated thus from the beginning. The whole notes in the flutes beginning at letter B were originally tied to each other, as were those in the flutes and double basses eight measures after B. On page 68, measures 10 and 11, the chorus was originally meant to join the solo voice in its crescendo and decrescendo; it may have covered the soloist too much, because the composer later crossed out this performance indication and added expressly: "< > gilt nur für die Solostimme" [< > holds only for the soloist]. On page 70, measure 6, the first flute was originally

then was changed and explicitly marked "Fl. col Oboe I." But two measures later this change is lacking, even though there seems to be no reason for it. For one thing, the bb^3 that would thereby be called for occurs often in the work, albeit as the highest flute tone; for another, on page 72, measures 2 and 6, flute and oboe moved in tandem from the outset. On page 83, measure 3, at the beginning of the movement's final section with the great pedal point on D, the various dynamic indications are the result of corrections that the composer later made, obviously after practical experience, to the *forte* originally required of all the instruments. The addition of *ma ben marcato* to the *fp* in the timpani is another of these; it appears in source A but is lacking in source B. The marking for the double bass was present from the beginning and affects that instrument only. Originally the cellos were to be divided, the second group doubling the double basses. In addition, the violins, violas, and first cellos were all to play legato to the end of the movement. The composer was careful to strike out the legato slurs throughout, and included the message to the engraver: "Die Bögen alle weg bis zum Schluss" [Remove all slurs up to the end]. By contrast, these slurs remained in the woodwinds. The horn pairs originally alternated in the following manner in holding the pedal point:

For the contrabassoon was written:

On page 87, measures 1–3, the bassoons held the low D (as on page 89, beginning at measure 3) and the clarinets remained silent until page 88, measure 1. One sees that the composer could not do enough to establish the pedal point. The fourth movement initially bore the tempo marking "Andante." In the last section of this movement the voices are led in octaves, an artistic device that Brahms seldom used and that in this passage bothered him increasingly in later years the more he heard the work. But because of the widespread popularity that it had by then achieved, he regarded any change as infeasible. The closing passage was originally only four measures long; the last two measures are a later addition. In the fifth movement, the composer first tried to give the first of the oboe solos to the bassoon an octave lower, but soon thought better of it; the first edition shows no sign of this change, which is so notable in the manuscript. In the sixth movement one finds in part the same notation for the clarinets as in the first movement. In the seventh movement (whose tempo marking was originally "Andante con moto"), as in the first movement, one passage that appears three times was later lengthened by one measure. From the sixth to the ninth measure, it proceeded as in Example 4; eight measures later [measure 14], as in Example 5; and at the repetition of this passage six measures after the A-major middle section [measure 107], as in Example 6. The choral passage that begins at letter A sounded originally as in Example 7, and the repetition of this passage after the above-mentioned middle section originally sounded as in Example 8—a change that is entered in the autograph score by a different hand, apparently at the behest of the composer, as the first edition shows. But even after publication of the work, Brahms indicated in his personal copy yet another practical change: from page 58, measure 7, to page 59, measure 3, he crossed out the legato of the *forte* ascending scales in the strings, obviously so that the violin notes could adequately penetrate through the constant *forte* of the other instruments. Finally it should be mentioned that on page 164, measure 6, and page 168, measure 6, the first note in the altos is g^1 in all the sources; the octaves with the bass and the bare choral setting on the strong part of the measure allow one to assume that this is a slip of the pen.

The illustrations that appear in this volume show how Brahms looked at the time he wrote the *German Requiem* and the style of his autography in this period; both are reproduced from originals in the collection of the Gesellschaft der Musikfreunde in Vienna.

Vienna
Spring, 1926   Eusebius Mandyczewski

Example (Beilage) 1

Example (Beilage) 2

Example (Beilage) 3

Example (Beilage) 4

Example (Beilage) 5

Example (Beilage) 6

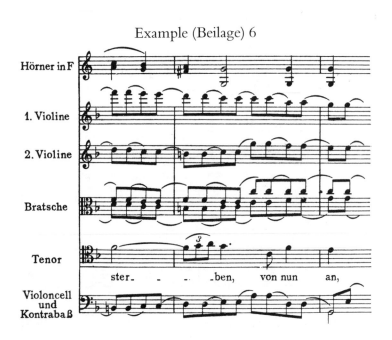

Example (Beilage) 7

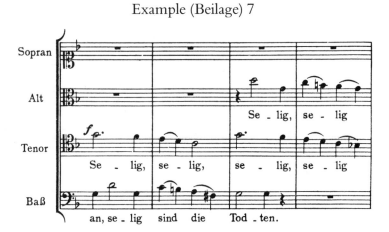

Example (Beilage) 8

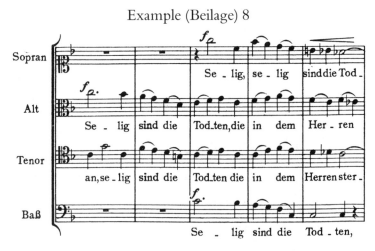

REVISIONSBERICHT

Für unsere Ausgabe dienten folgende im Besitze der Gesellschaft der Musikfreunde in Wien befindlichen Vorlagen:

A. Die Handschrift des Komponisten;

B. die erste Ausgabe, Handexemplar des Komponisten;

C. die Stimmen, die bei den ersten Wiener Aufführungen unter der Leitung des Komponisten benutzt wurden.

A. Die Handschrift, auf sieben Bogenlagen (für jeden Satz eine) in Hochformat geschrieben, trägt auf der ersten Seite kurz gefaßt den Titel: ›**Ein deutsches Requiem. J. B.**‹

1. Satz: 12 Blätter 14 zeiliges Papier, nach dem 9. Blatt ein eingelegtes Blatt 18 zeiliges Papier mit den nachträglichen Veränderungen. Titel: ›Selig sind, die da Leid tragen.‹

2. Satz: 12 Blätter 20 zeiliges Papier, 4 Blätter 20 zeiliges Papier von anderem Format, 4 Blätter 18 zeiliges Papier, nach dem 16. Blatt ein halbes Blatt als Einlage mit der nachträglichen Veränderung. Titel: ›Denn alles Fleisch ist wie Gras.‹

3. Satz: 18 Blätter 20 zeiliges Papier. Titel: ›Herr, lehre doch mich.‹

4. Satz: (ursprünglich mit Nr. 5 bezeichnet): 12 Blätter 18 zeiliges Papier. Titel: ›Wie lieblich sind deine Wohnungen.‹

5. Satz: 8 Blätter 18 zeiliges Papier. Titel: ›Ihr habt nun Traurigkeit.‹

6. Satz: 8 Blätter 18 zeiliges Papier, 24 Blätter 20 zeiliges Papier. Titel: ›Denn wir haben hie.‹

7. Satz: 14 Blätter 20 zeiliges Papier. Titel: ›Selig sind die Todten‹. Am Schluß notiert der Komponist: ›Baden-Baden im Sommer 1866.‹

Die aus den Anfangsworten der Texte herrührenden Titel der einzelnen Sätze hat der Verleger gestrichen, gewiß nur im Einverständnis mit dem Komponisten, hat auf der ersten Seite Anweisungen für den Stich gegeben, und den Text in allen Sätzen dort ergänzt, wo er als selbstverständlich noch nicht stand. So konnte die Handschrift als Vorlage für den Stich dienen, wie auch aus der Platteneinteilung ersichtlich ist, die sie trägt. In dieser Vorlage stehen die Singstimmen in den Gesangschlüsseln, und es fehlen die Partien der ad libitum zu verwendenden Instrumente: Kontrafagott und Orgel, deren Einsätze nur nachträglich vom Komponisten vermerkt sind.

B. Die erste Ausgabe erschien 1868 bei Rieter-Biedermann (jetzt C. F. Peters) in Leipzig unter dem Titel: ›Ein deutsches Requiem nach Worten der Heiligen Schrift für Soli, Chor und Orchester (Orgel ad libitum) von Johannes Brahms op. 45. Partitur. Klavierauszug mit Text. Klavierauszug zu vier Händen. Chor- und Orchesterstimmen.‹ Verlagsnummer 592—596. In der Partitur fehlt die Orgelpartie; ihr Eintreten und Aussetzen ist bei der Kontrabaßpartie mit ›Org. t. s.‹, ›con Org.‹, ›Org. tacet‹ angegeben. Eine vom Komponisten vollständig ausgearbeitete Orgelstimme ist aber den Orchesterstimmen beigegeben. Dagegen wissen weder Partitur noch Stimmen etwas vom Kontrafagott. In seinem Handexemplar der Partitur hat aber der Komponist nachträglich mit Blaustift das Ein- und Aussetzen dieses Instruments angegeben; ›c. Vc.‹, ›c. B.‹, ›tac.‹ besagt, wo und wie weit es mit Violoncell oder Kontrabaß gehen soll.

C. Die vom Komponisten benutzten alten Wiener Orchesterstimmen enthalten eine mit den Angaben der genannten Vorlagen übereinstimmende geschriebene Kontrafagottstimme. Daß sie nicht ausdrücklich als ad libitum zu verwendende Stimme bezeichnet ist, mag eine Flüchtigkeit des Notenschreibers gewesen sein. Obligat ist sie nicht, wie aus dem Gesagten und aus ihrer Beschaffenheit erhellt.

Im einzelnen verrät die Vorlage A, daß der Komponist an seinem Werke auch nach der Vollendung gefeilt und verbessert hat. Es ist bekannt, daß er nie etwas veröffentlicht hat, ohne es gehört zu haben. Und so dürften auch die Veränderungen im Deutschen Requiem auf die Wirkung der ersten Proben zurückzuführen sein. Zunächst fallen im 1. Satz zwei Erweiterungen auf: die zehn Takte, die dem Buchstaben E folgen, sind an Stelle der fünf Takte gesetzt worden, die wir in der Beilage 1 mitteilen; die zehn Takte, die Seite 17, Takt 5 anfangen, sind aus den sieben in Beilage 2 mitgeteilten Takten entstanden. Für den Anfang des 2. Satzes war ursprünglich bloß piano, mezza voce und legato vorgeschrieben, den Streichern legato e dolce. Daß diese Bezeichnung nicht ausreichte, haben gewiß die Proben erwiesen. Der etwas bewegtere Mittelsatz in Gesdur war ursprünglich ohne Harfe. Nach der Wiederholung des 1. Teils sollte der B dur-Satz (Buchstabe H) Un poco animato anfangen. Drei Takte vor dem Buchstaben M hat der Komponist nachträglich einen Takt eingeschoben; unsere Beilage 3 zeigt die ursprüngliche Fassung dieser Stelle. Im 3. Satz fällt zunächst die Notierung der Klarinetten auf; sie war von Anfang an so. Die beim Buchstaben B einsetzenden ganzen Noten der Flöten waren ursprünglich an einander gebunden; ebenso acht Takte später die der Flöten und Streicherbässe. Seite 68, Takt 10 und 11 sollte der Chor ursprünglich das crescendo und decrescendo der Singstimme mitmachen; er mag sie zu sehr gedeckt haben, denn der Komponist streicht nachträglich diese Vortragszeichen und setzt ausdrücklich hinzu: ›< > gilt nur für die Solostimme.‹

Seite 70, Takt 6 erste Flöte ursprünglich , dann geändert und ausdrücklich bemerkt ›Fl. col Oboe I‹. Aber zwei Takte später fehlt diese Änderung, obwohl dafür kein Grund vorliegt, da einerseits das b^3, das dadurch gefordert würde, in dem

Werke öfter vorkommt, wenn auch als der höchste Flötenton, andrerseits Seite 72, Takt 2 und 6 Flöte und Oboe schon ursprünglich zusammengingen. Seite 83, Takt 3, beim Eintritt der Schlußpartie dieses Satzes mit dem großen Orgelpunkt auf *D*, sind die verschiedenen dynamischen Bezeichnungen aus Korrekturen hervorgegangen, die der Komponist nachträglich, offenbar nach praktischer Erfahrung, an dem ursprünglich von allen Instrumenten verlangten forte vorgenommen hat. Das dem *fp* der Pauke beigefügte »ma ben marcato« gehört auch dazu. Es steht in der Vorlage A, fehlt aber in der Vorlage B. Die Bemerkung zum Kontrabaß stand von allem Anfang an da und gilt nur für ihn. Ursprünglich sollten die Violoncelle geteilt werden, das zweite mit dem zweiten Kontrabaß gehn. Ebenso sollten die Violinen, Violen und ersten Violoncelle alles bis zum Schluß des Satzes legato spielen. Die legato-Bogen hat der Komponist überall peinlich genau gestrichen und für den Stecher die Bemerkung hinzugesetzt: »Die Bögen alle weg bis zum Schluß«. Dagegen blieben diese Bogen bei den Holzblasinstrumenten. Die Hörnerpaare sollten sich ursprünglich im Aushalten des Orgelpunktes folgendermaßen ablösen:

für das Kontrafagott war vorgeschrieben:

Seite 87, Takt 1 bis 3 hielten die Fagotte das *D* aus (wie Seite 89, Takt 3 u. f.) und die Klarinetten pausierten bis Seite 88, Takt 1. Man sieht, der Komponist konnte sich im Orgelpunkt gar nicht genug tun. Der 4. Satz trug anfangs die Tempobezeichnung Andante. In der Schlußpartie dieses Satzes werden die Singstimmen in Oktaven geführt, ein Kunstmittel, das Brahms nur selten anwendet, und das ihn an dieser Stelle in späteren Jahren immer mehr gestört hat, je öfter er das Werk hörte. Aber bei der Verbreitung und Beliebtheit, die es inzwischen erreicht hatte, hielt er eine Änderung für untunlich. Das Nachspiel war ursprünglich viertaktig; die letzten zwei Takte sind eine spätere Zutat. Im 5. Satz machte der Komponist den Versuch, das erste der Oboe zugeteilte Solo eine Oktave tiefer dem Fagott zu geben, stand aber bald davon wieder ab. Denn von dieser in der Handschrift bemerkbaren Veränderung weiß die erste Ausgabe nichts. Im 6. Satz findet sich zum Teil dieselbe Notierung der Klarinetten wie im 3. Satz. Im 7. Satz, dessen Tempobezeichnung ursprünglich Andante con moto war, ist, wie im 1. Satz, an einer dreimal vorkommenden Stelle eine nachträgliche Erweiterung um einen Takt bemerkbar; vom 6. zum 9. Takt ging es wie Beilage 4 zeigt, acht Takte später wie in Beilage 5 und bei der Wiederholung dieser Stelle, sechs Takte nach dem Adur-Mittelsatz, wie in Beilage 6 zu sehen ist. Der beim Buchstaben A eintretende Chorsatz lautete ursprünglich wie wir in Beilage 7, für die Wiederholung dieser Stelle nach dem erwähnten Mittelsatz in Beilage 8 mitteilen, eine Veränderung, die in der autographen Partitur von fremder Hand eingetragen ist, offenbar über Anordnung des Komponisten, wie die erste Ausgabe zeigt. Aber auch nach der Veröffentlichung des Werkes hat Brahms in seinem Handexemplar noch eine praktische Änderung angegeben und Seite 58, Takt 7 bis Seite 59, Takt 3 das legato der im forte aufsteigenden Tonleitern der Streichinstrumente gestrichen, offenbar, damit die Töne der Geigen im steten forte der übrigen Stimmen genügend durchdringen. Endlich sei erwähnt, daß Seite 164, Takt 6 und Seite 168, Takt 6 die erste Note im Alt in allen Vorlagen *g*[1] ist; die Oktaven mit dem Baß und der leere Chorsatz auf dem guten Taktteil ließen annehmen, daß ein Schreibversehen vorliegt.

Die Beilagen, die diesem Bande beigegeben sind, zeigen, wie Brahms aussah, als er das »Deutsche Requiem« schrieb, und wie seine Schriftzüge in dieser Zeit waren; beide nach Vorlagen im Besitze der Gesellschaft der Musikfreunde in Wien.

Wien, im Frühjahr 1926.

E usebius Mandyczewski.

Instrumentation

Piccolo [Kleine Flöte]
2 Flutes [Flöten]
2 Oboes [Oboen]
2 Clarinets [Klarinetten] (A, B♭)
2 Bassoons [Fagotte]
Contrabassoon [Kontrafagott] ad libitum

4 Horns [Hörner] (F, B♭ basso, C basso, D, E♭, E)
2 Trumpets [Trompeten] (B♭, D, C)
3 Trombones [Posaunen]
Tuba [Tuba]

3 Timpani [Pauken]

Harp [Harfe] (doubled at least)

Violins [Violine] I, II
Violas [Bratschen]
Cellos [Violoncell]
Basses [Kontrabass]

Organ [Orgel] ad libitum

Soprano [Sopran] Solo
Bass [Bass]-Baritone [Bariton] Solo

Sopranos [Sopran]
Altos [Alt]
Tenors [Tenor]
Bass [Bass]

Ein deutsches Requiem

1

Selig sind, die da Leid tragen, denn sie sollen getröstet werden. *Matth. 5, 4.*

Die mit Tränen säen, werden mit Freuden ernten.

Sie gehen hin und weinen und tragen edlen Samen, und kommen mit Freuden und bringen ihre Garben. *Ps. 126, 5. 6.*

2

Denn alles Fleisch ist wie Gras und alle Herrlichkeit des Menschen wie des Grases Blumen. Das Gras ist verdorret und die Blume abgefallen. *1. Petri 1, 24.*

So seid nun geduldig, lieben Brüder, bis auf die Zukunft des Herrn. Siehe, ein Ackermann wartet auf die köstliche Frucht der Erde und ist geduldig darüber, bis er empfahe den Morgenregen und Abendregen. *Jacobi 5, 7.*

Aber des Herrn Wort bleibet in Ewigkeit. *1. Petri 1, 25.*

Die Erlöseten des Herrn werden wieder kommen, und gen Zion kommen mit Jauchzen; ewige Freude wird über ihrem Haupte sein; Freude und Wonne werden sie ergreifen und Schmerz und Seufzen wird weg müssen. *Jesaias 35, 10.*

3

Herr, lehre doch mich, daß ein Ende mit mir haben muß, und mein Leben ein Ziel hat, und ich davon muß.

Siehe, meine Tage sind einer Hand breit vor dir, und mein Leben ist wie nichts vor dir.

Ach wie gar nichts sind alle Menschen, die doch so sicher leben. Sie gehen daher wie ein Schemen, und machen ihnen viel vergebliche Unruhe; sie sammeln und wissen nicht wer es kriegen wird. Nun Herr, wess soll ich mich trösten? Ich hoffe auf dich. *Ps. 39, 5. 6. 7. 8.*

Der Gerechten Seelen sind in Gottes Hand und keine Qual rühret sie an. *Weish. Sal. 3, 1.*

4

Wie lieblich sind deine Wohnungen, Herr Zebaoth! Meine Seele verlanget und sehnet sich nach den Vorhöfen des Herrn; mein Leib und Seele freuen sich in dem lebendigen Gott. Wohl denen, die in deinem Hause wohnen, die loben dich immerdar. *Ps. 84, 2. 3. 5.*

5

Ihr habt nun Traurigkeit; aber ich will euch wieder sehen und euer Herz soll sich freuen und eure Freude soll niemand von euch nehmen. *Ev. Joh. 16, 22.*

Sehet mich an: Ich habe eine kleine Zeit Mühe und Arbeit gehabt und habe großen Trost funden. *Sirach 51, 35.*

Ich will euch trösten, wie Einen seine Mutter tröstet. *Jes. 66, 13.*

6

Denn wir haben hie keine bleibende Statt, sondern die zukünftige suchen wir. *Ebr. 13, 14.*

Siehe, ich sage euch ein Geheimnis: Wir werden nicht alle entschlafen, wir werden aber alle verwandelt werden; und dasselbige plötzlich, in einem Augenblick, zu der Zeit der letzten Posaune. Denn es wird die Posaune schallen, und die Toten werden auferstehen unverweslich, und wir werden verwandelt werden. Dann wird erfüllet werden das Wort, das geschrieben steht: Der Tod ist verschlungen in den Sieg. Tod, wo ist dein Stachel? Hölle, wo ist dein Sieg? *1. Korinther 15, 51-55.*

Herr, du bist würdig zu nehmen Preis und Ehre und Kraft, denn du hast alle Dinge geschaffen, und durch deinen Willen haben sie das Wesen und sind geschaffen. *Off. Joh. 4, 11.*

7

Selig sind die Toten, die in dem Herrn sterben, von nun an. Ja der Geist spricht, daß sie ruhen von ihrer Arbeit; denn ihre Werke folgen ihnen nach. *Off. Joh. 14, 13.*

A German Requiem

[The following translations are taken from the King James Version of the Bible.]

1

Blessed are they that mourn: for they shall be comforted.   Matthew 5:4

They that sow in tears shall reap in joy.

He that goeth forth and weepeth, bearing precious seed, shall doubtless come again with rejoicing, bringing his sheaves with him.   Psalm 126:5,6

2

For all flesh is as grass, and all the glory of man as the flower of grass. The grass withereth, and the flower thereof falleth away.   1 Peter 1:24

Be patient therefore, brethren, unto the coming of the Lord. Behold, the husbandman waiteth for the precious fruit of the earth, and hath long patience for it, until he receive the early and latter rain.   James 5:7

But the word of the Lord endureth for ever. 1 Peter 1:25

And the ransomed of the Lord shall return, and come to Zion with songs and everlasting joy upon their heads: they shall obtain joy and gladness, and sorrow and sighing shall flee away.   Isaiah 35:10

3

Lord, make me to know mine end, and the measure of my days, what it is: that I may know how frail I am.

Behold, thou hast made my days as an handbreadth; and mine age is as nothing before thee. . . .

Surely every man walketh in a vain shew: surely they are disquieted in vain: he heapeth up riches, and knoweth not who shall gather them.

And now, Lord, what wait I for? my hope is in thee.   Psalm 39:4–7

But the souls of the righteous are in the hand of God, and there shall no torment touch them.   Wisdom of Solomon 3:1

4

How amiable are thy tabernacles, O Lord of hosts!

My soul longeth, yea, even fainteth for the courts of the Lord: my heart and my flesh crieth out for the living God.

Blessed are they that dwell in thy house: they will be still praising thee.   Psalm 84:1,2,4

5

And ye now therefore have sorrow: but I will see you again, and your heart shall rejoice, and your joy no man taketh from you.   John 16:22

Ye see how for a little while I labor and toil, yet have I found much rest.   Ecclesiasticus 51:27

As one whom his mother comforteth, so will I comfort you. . . .   Isaiah 66:13

6

For here have we no continuing city, but we seek one to come.   Hebrews 13:14

Behold, I shew you a mystery; We shall not all sleep, but we shall all be changed,

In a moment, in the twinkling of an eye, at the last trump: for the trumpet shall sound, and the dead shall be raised incorruptible, and we shall be changed.

. . . then shall be brought to pass the saying that is written, Death is swallowed up in victory.

O death, where is thy sting? O grave, where is thy victory?   1 Corinthians 15:51,52,54,55

Thou art worthy, O Lord, to receive glory and honour and power: for thou hast created all things, and for thy pleasure they are and were created.   Revelation 4:11

7

. . . Blessed are the dead which die in the Lord from henceforth: Yea, saith the Spirit, that they may rest from their labours; and their works do follow them.   Revelation 14:13

FIRST ENTRANCE OF THE CHORUS: AUTOGRAPH MANUSCRIPT.

———

GERMAN REQUIEM

A GERMAN REQUIEM
to Words of Holy Scripture
for Soloists, Chorus and Orchestra (Organ ad lib.)

1   Selig sind, die da Leid tragen

2 Denn alles Fleisch es ist wie Gras

kl. Fl.
Fl.
Ob.
Klar. (B)
Fag.
K-Fag.
Hr. (B)
Hr. (C)
Trpt. (B)
Pos.
3. Pos. Tuba
Pk.
169
Harfe
poco a poco cresc.
mf cresc.
mf sempre cresc.
p cresc.
sempre cresc.
mf
cresc.

H Un poco sostenuto

Allegro non troppo

Allegro non troppo

3 Herr, lehre doch mich

Andante moderato

2 Flöten
2 Oboen
2 Klarinetten in A
2 Fagotte
Kontrafagott (ad lib.)
2 Hörner in D
2 Hörner in tief B
2 Trompeten in D
1.u.2. Posaune
3. Posaune u. Tuba
Pauken in D A

Baß-Solo

Herr, lehre doch mich, daß ein En _ de mit mir ha _ ben muß, und mein Le _ ben ein Ziel hat,

Sopran
Alt
Tenor
Baß

1.Violine
2.Violine
Bratsche
Violoncell
Kontrabaß

Orgel (ad lib.)

Andante moderato

und ich da _ von muß, und ich da _ von __ muß.

Herr, leh _ re doch mich, daß ein En _ _ de mit mir

Herr, leh _ re doch mich, daß ein En _ _ de mit mir

Herr, Herr, leh _ re doch mich, daß ein En _ _ de mit mir

Herr, Herr, leh _ re doch mich, daß ein En _ _ de mit mir

Sie_he, mei_ne Ta _ ge sind ei_ne Hand breit vor dir,_____ und mein Le _ ben

Herr, leh_re doch mich, daß ein En _ de mit mir

wie nichts vor dir.

wie nichts vor dir.

wie nichts vor dir.

wie nichts vor dir.

ha _ ben muß, und mein Le _ ben ein Ziel hat, und ich da _ von muß, und ich da _ von

Ach,— wie gar nichts sind—— al_le Men_schen, die doch so

Sie ge_hen da_her wie ein Sche _ _ _ men, und machen ih _ _ nen viel ver_geb_li_che Un_

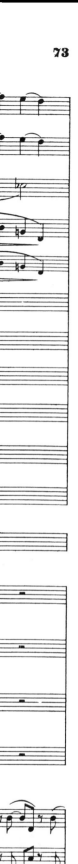

ru_he; sie sammeln, und wissen nicht wer es kriegen wird.

Ach,_____ wie_ gar nichts

Ach,_____ wie_ gar nichts

Ach,_____ wie_ gar nichts

Ach,_____ wie_ gar nichts

4 Wie lieblich sind deine Wohnungen

5   Ihr habt nun Traurigkeit

keit; a_ _ber, a_ _ber ich will euch wieder se_hen und euer Herz soll sich freuen, und

Ich will_ euch

Ich will_ euch

Ich will euch

Ich will_ euch

Se _ het mich an: ich ha _ be ei _ ne klei _ ne Zeit Mü _ he und Ar _ beit ge _ habt und ha _ be

Ihr ____ habt nun Trau _ _ _ _ rig _ keit, ihr habt nun Trau _ _ rig-keit,

6 Denn wir haben hie keine bleibende Statt

Siehe, ich sage euch ein Ge- heim - - - - nis: Wir wer- den nicht al - le ent- schla -

Dann, dann wird er fül _ let wer _ den das Wort, das ge _ schrie _ ben

Allegro

Allegro

7 Selig sind die Toten

186

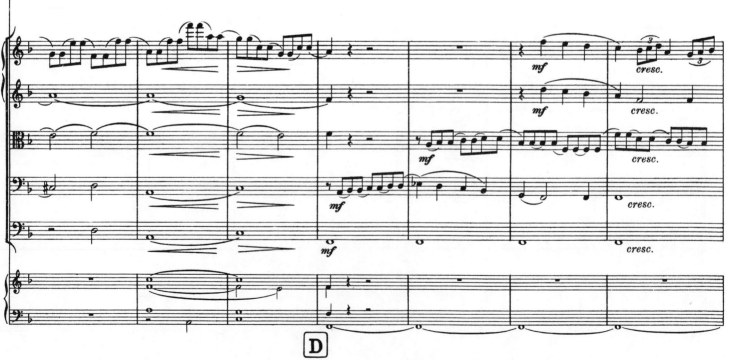